NOD'S DREAM

by J.M.S. Asbury

Published by:
Jaz Books,
34 Penn Grove Road,
Hereford.

Copyright © J.M.S. Asbury 1993

First Edition

ISBN   0952 1815 0 9

Printed by:
Apple Press,
Mortimer Road,
Hereford.

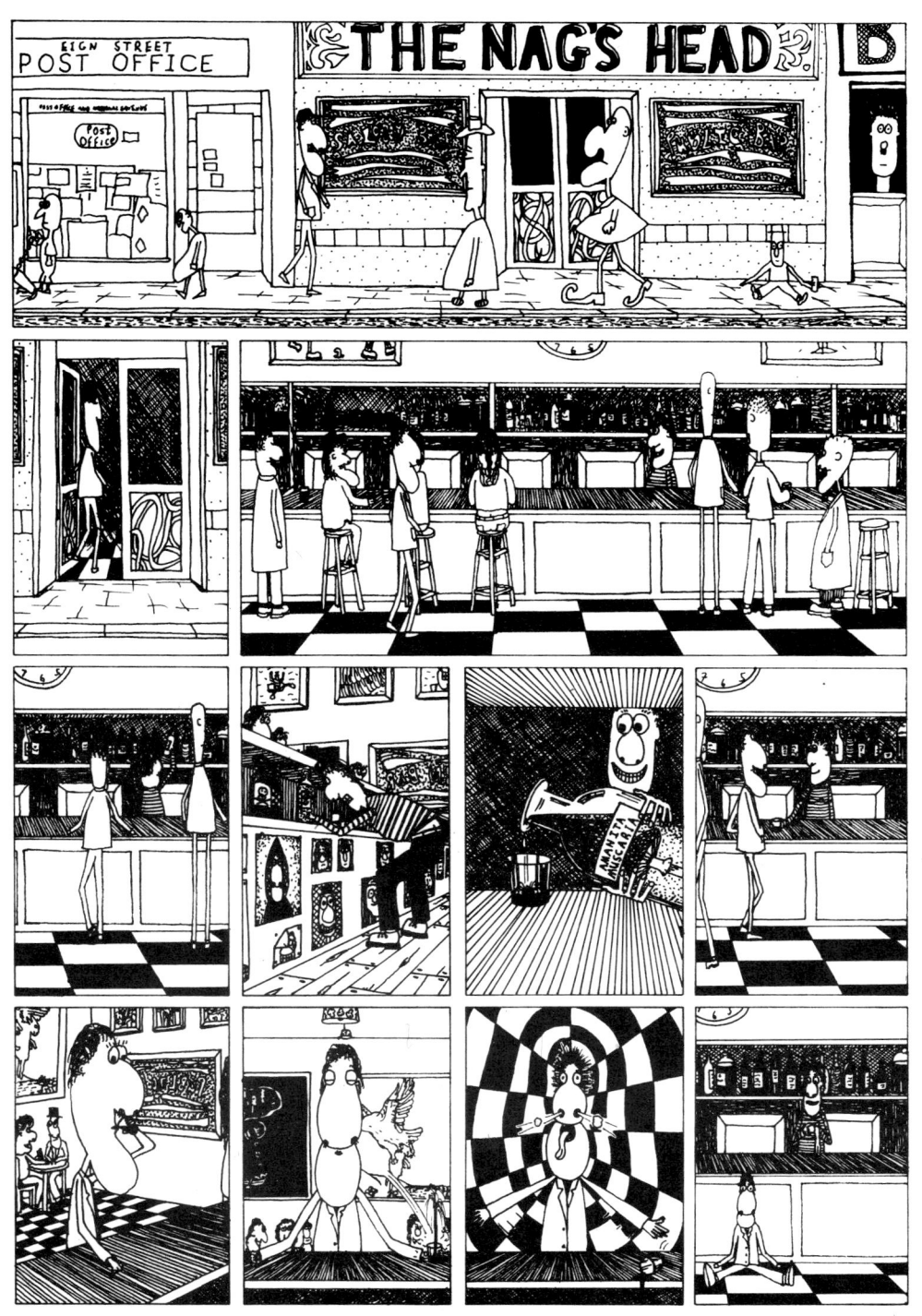

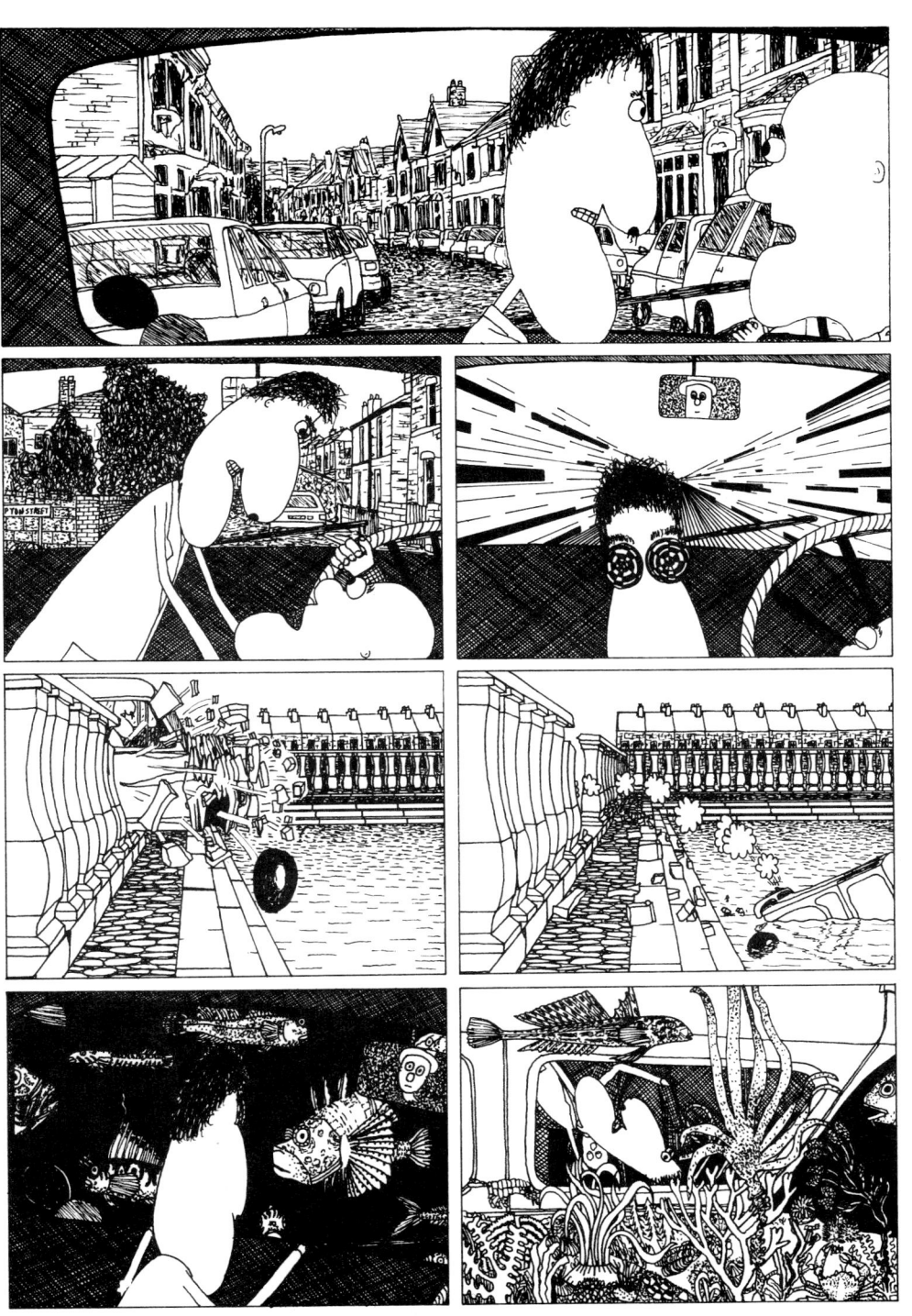

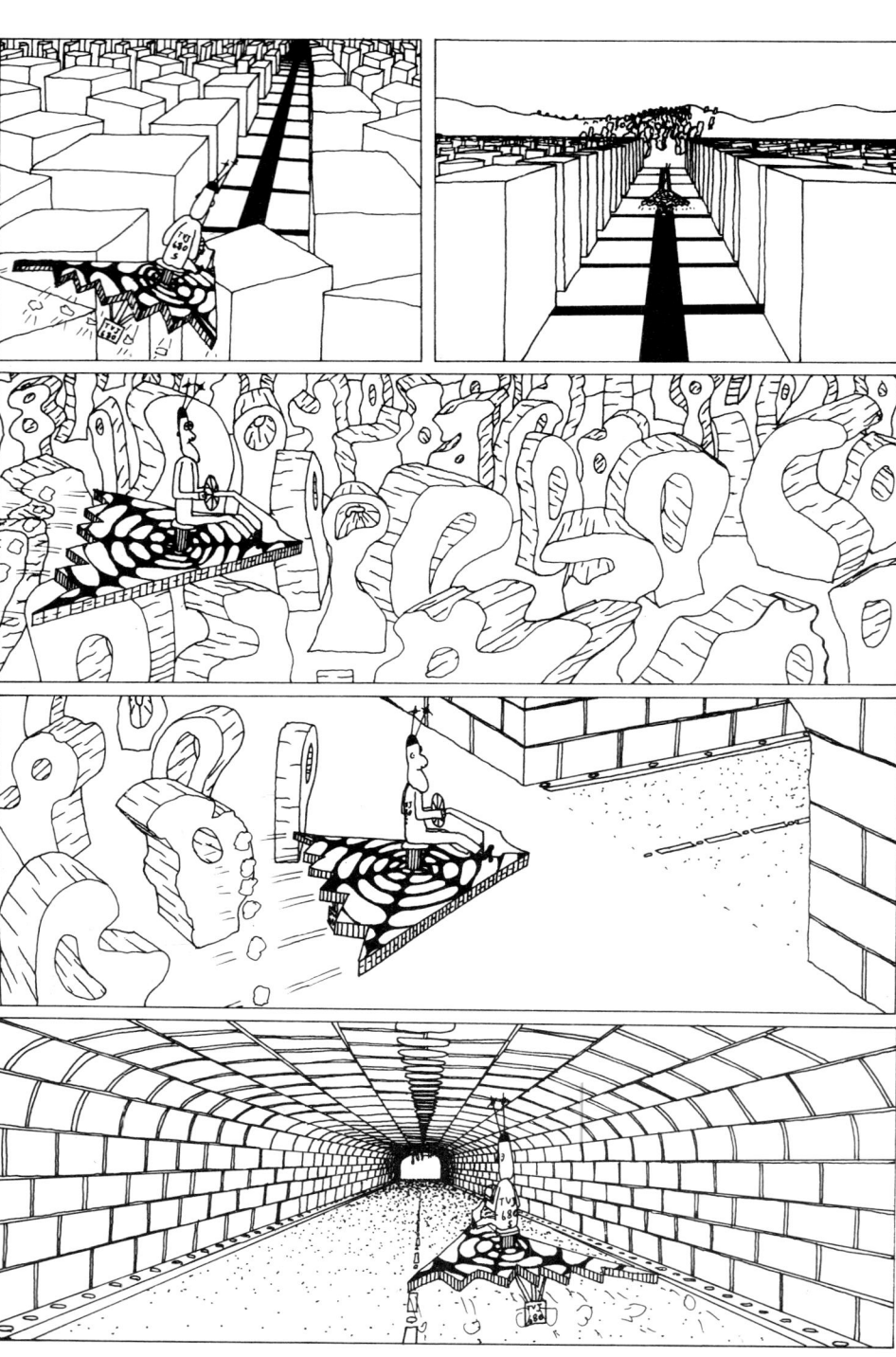

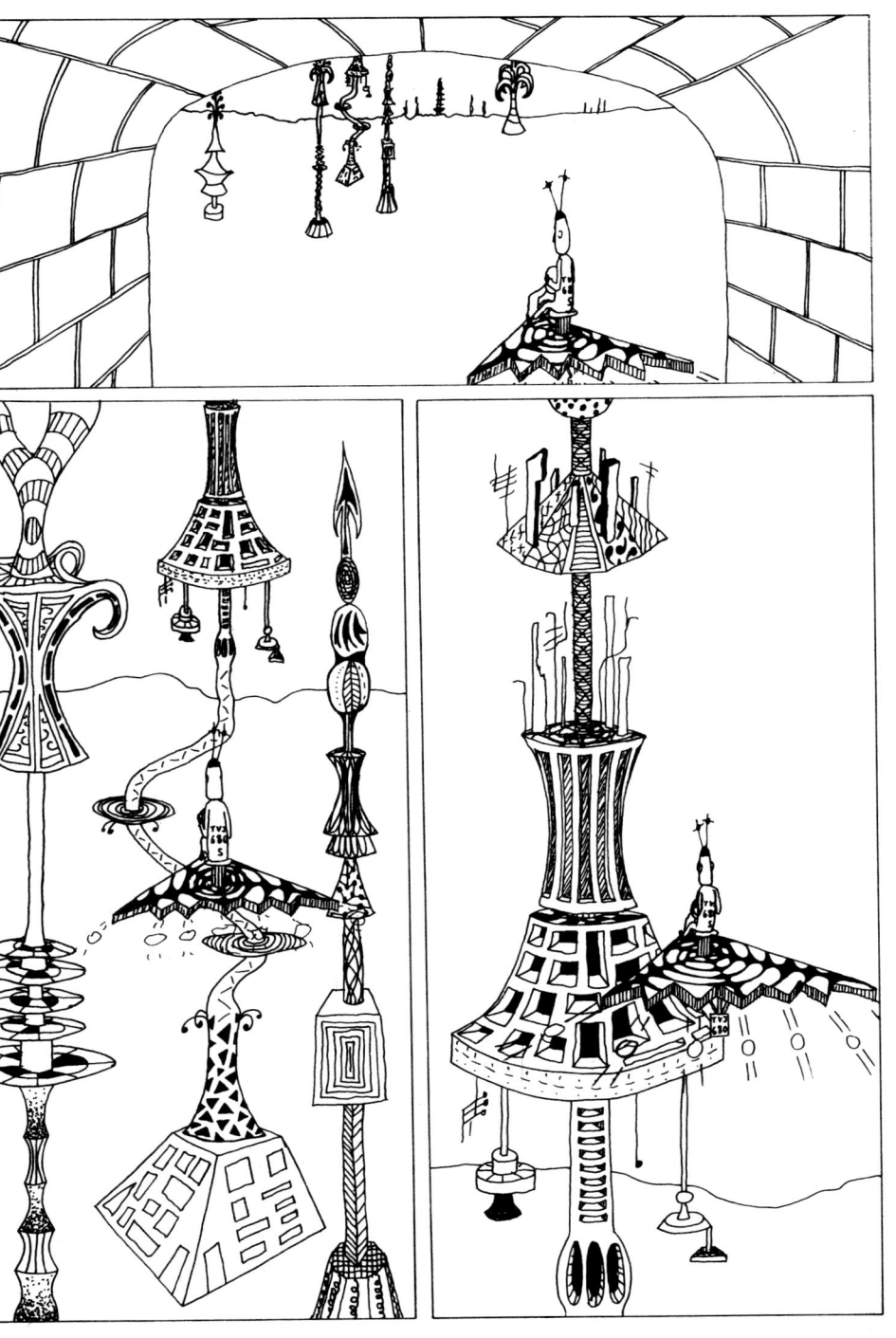

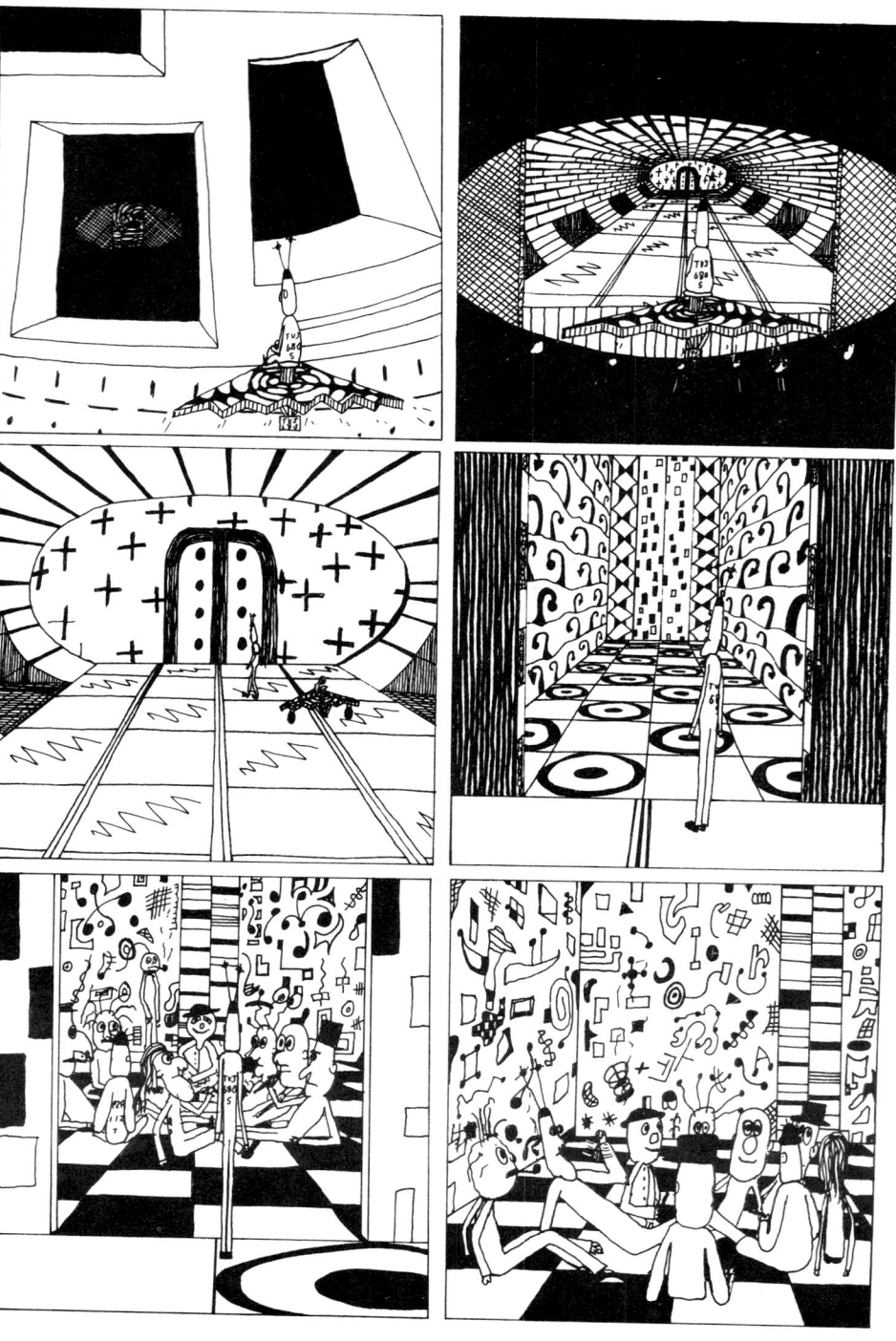

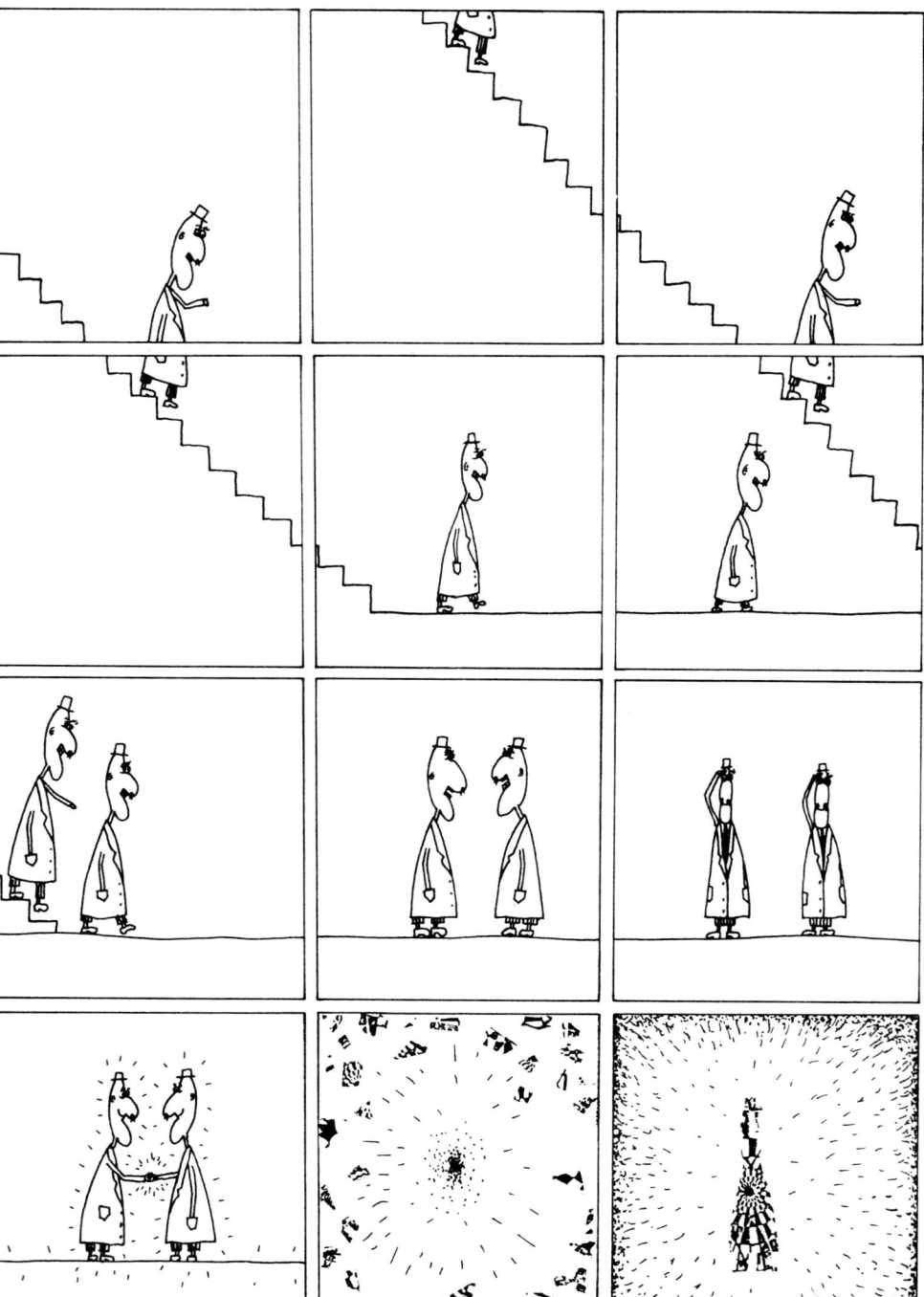

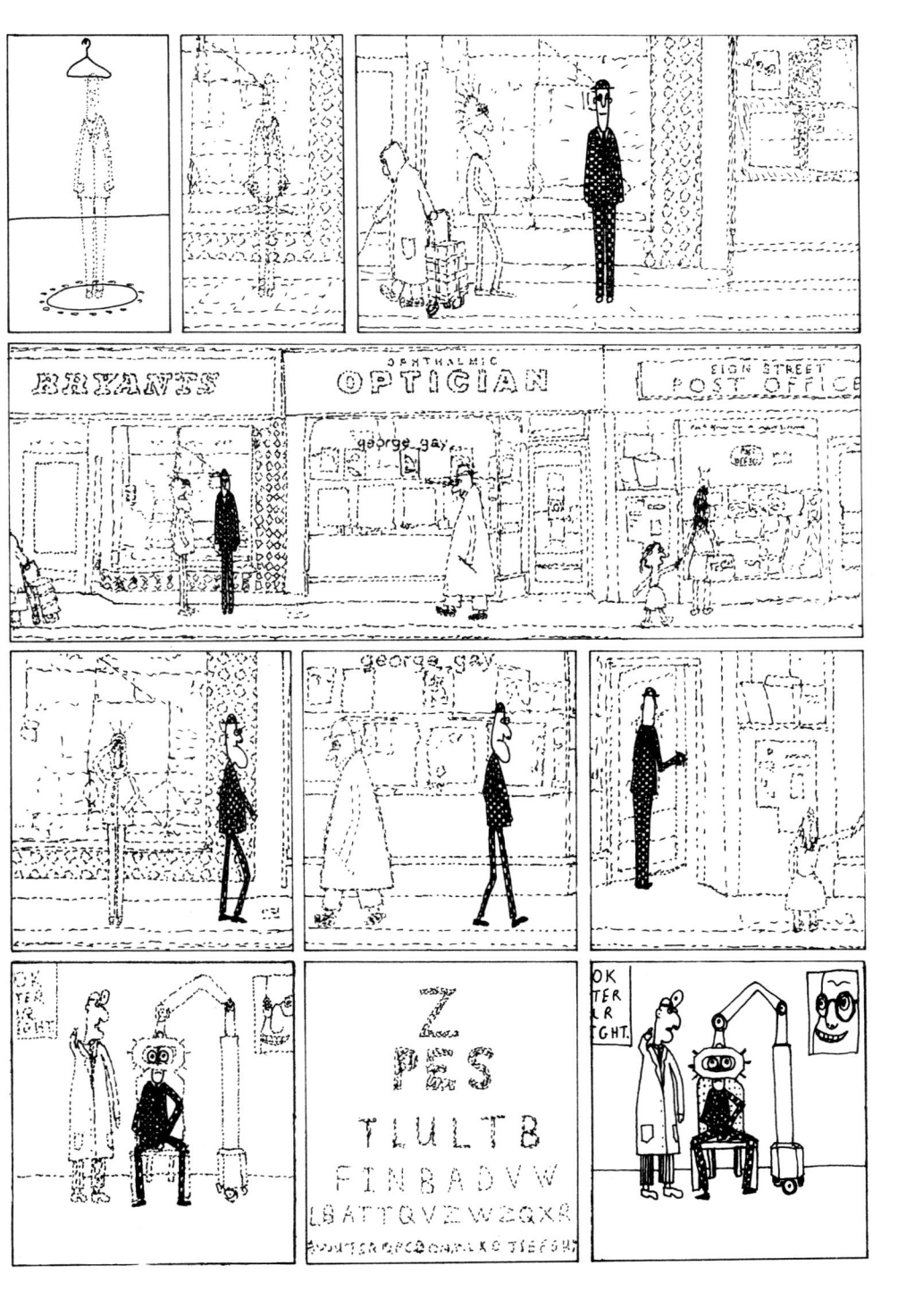

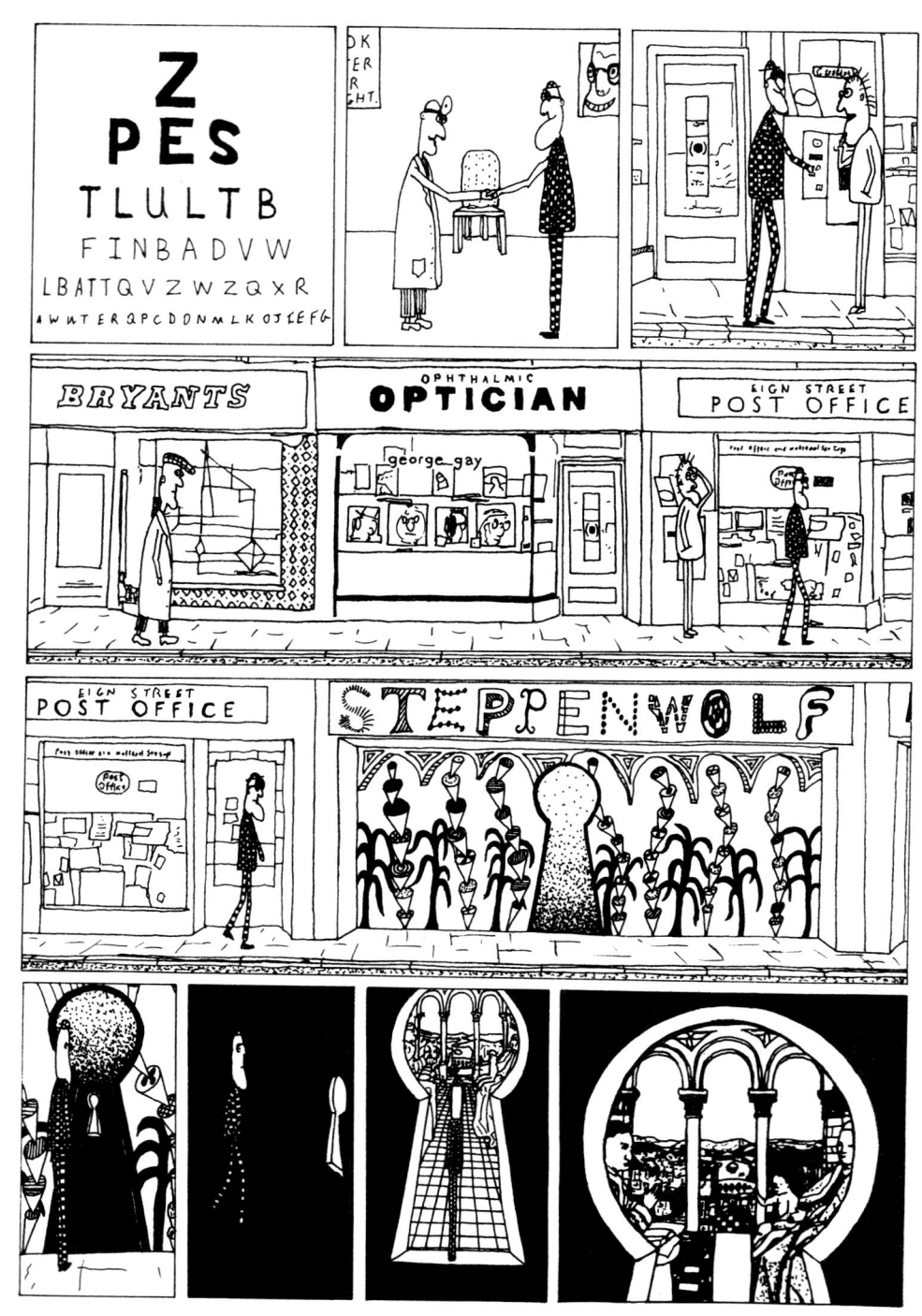

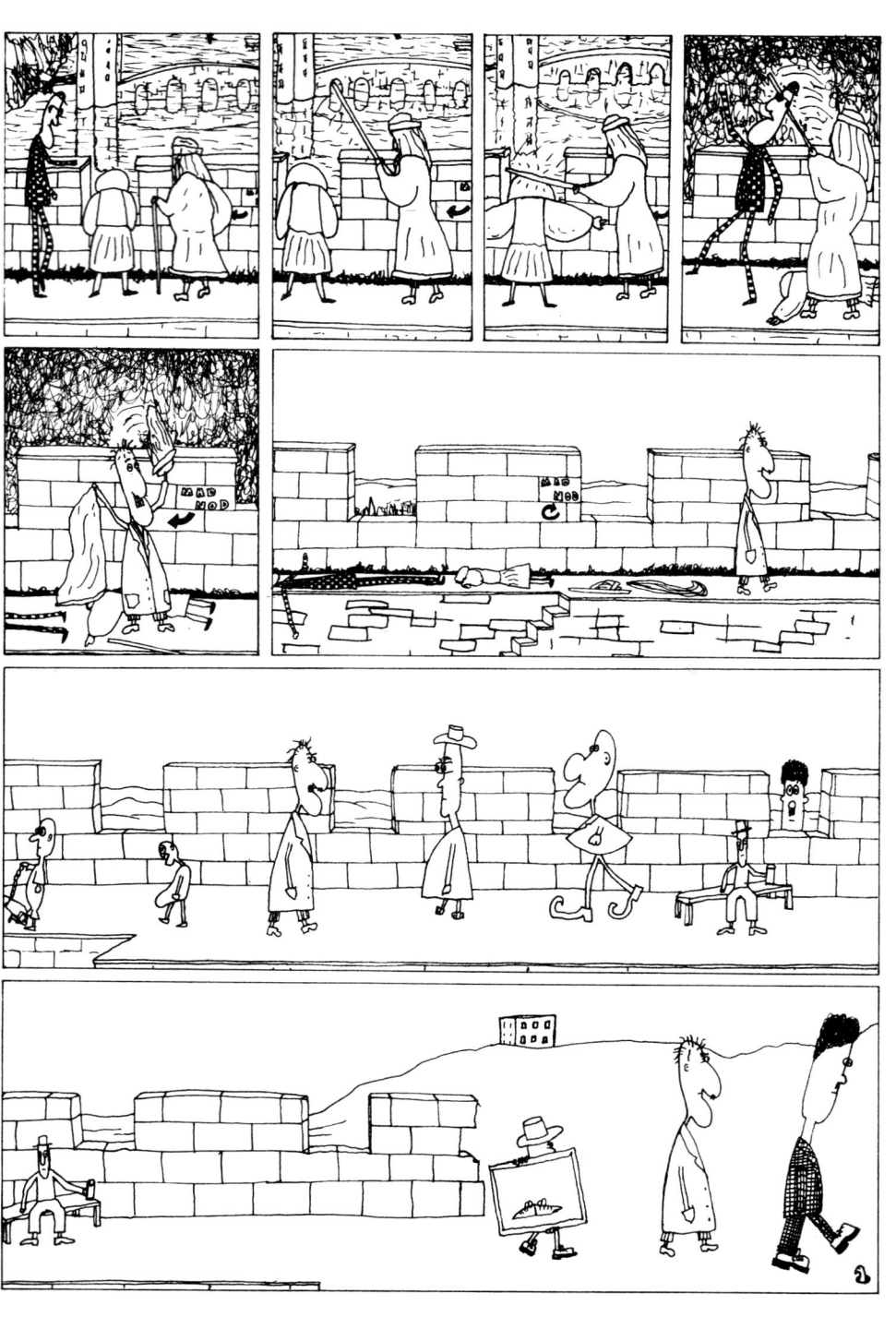

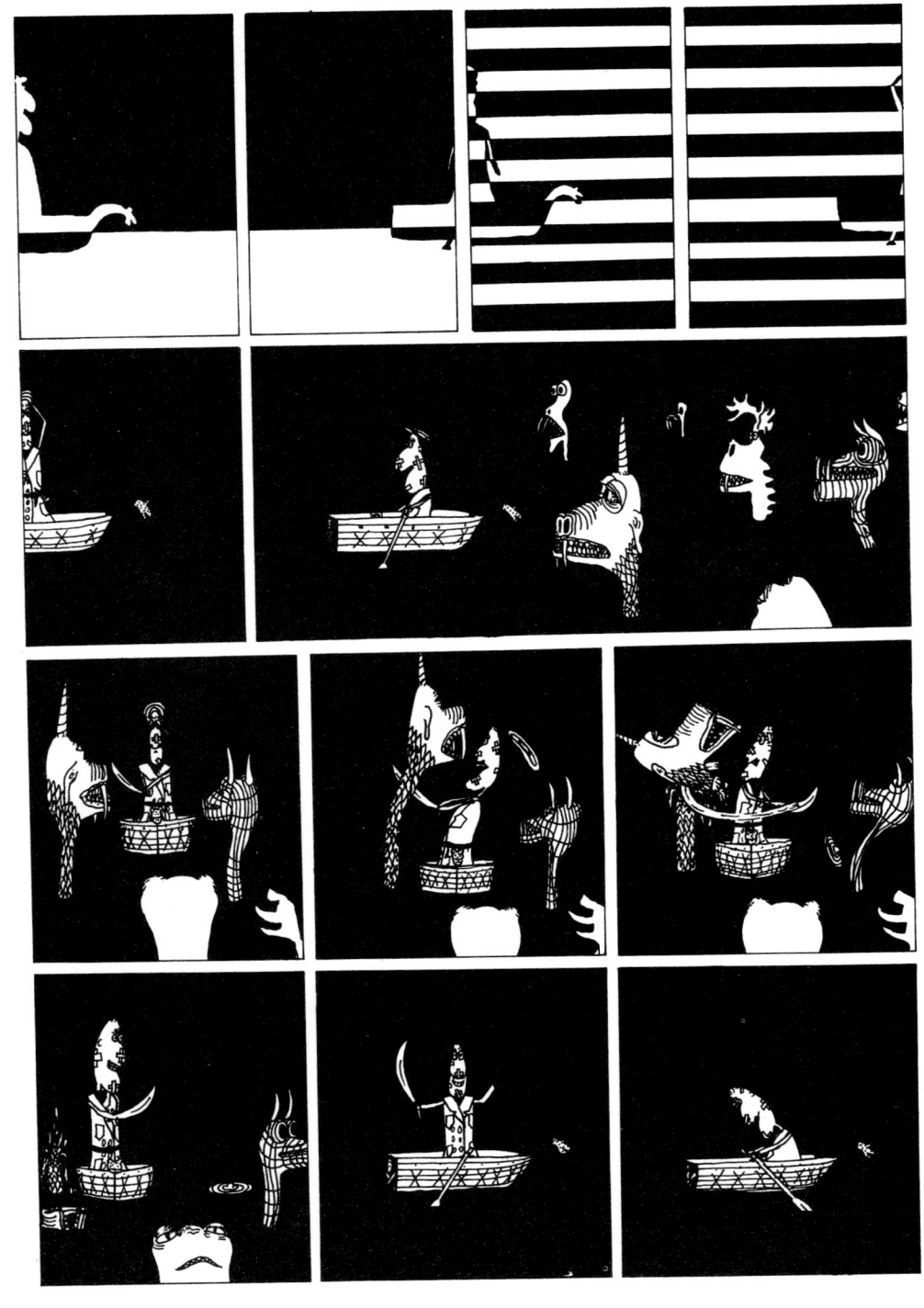

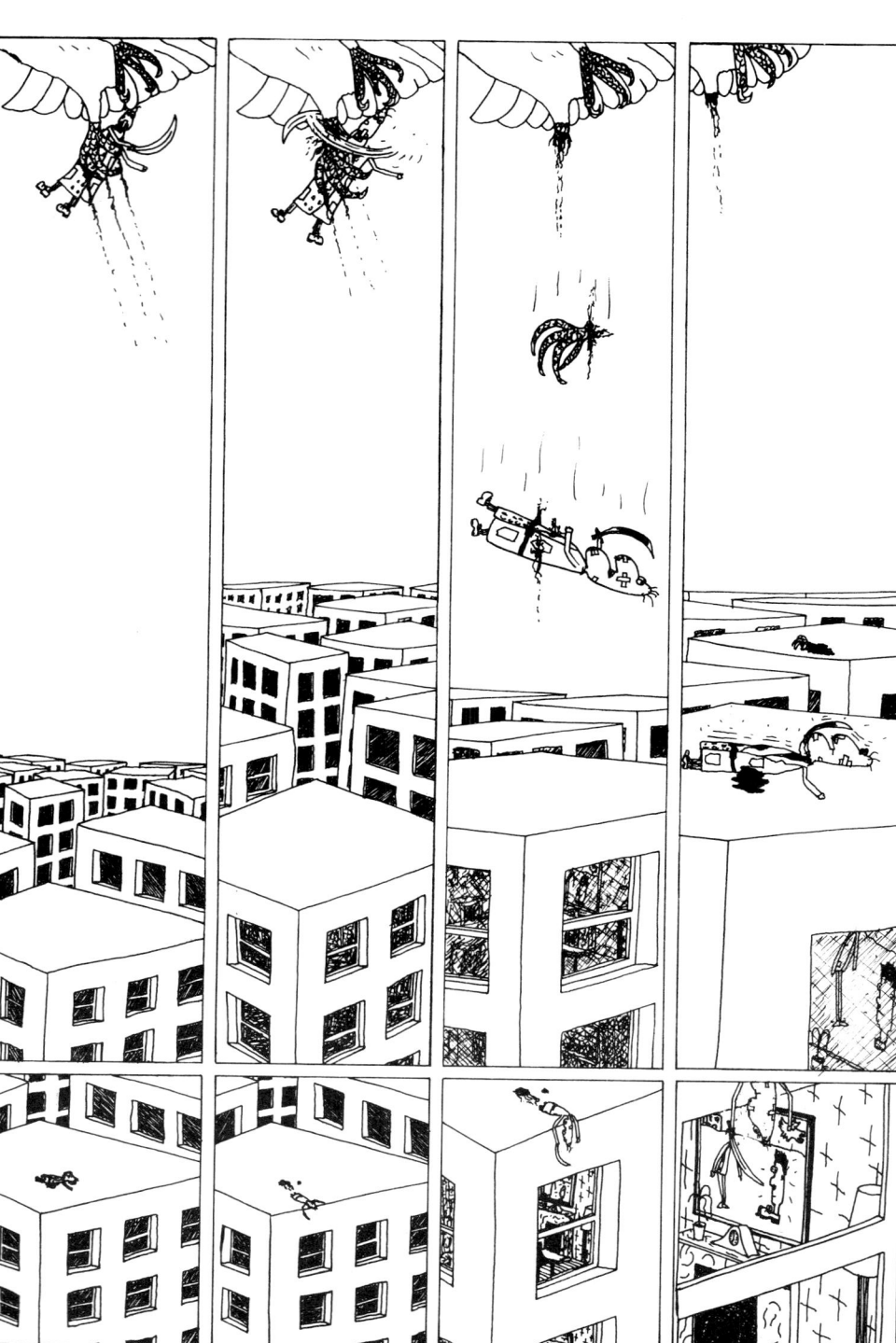

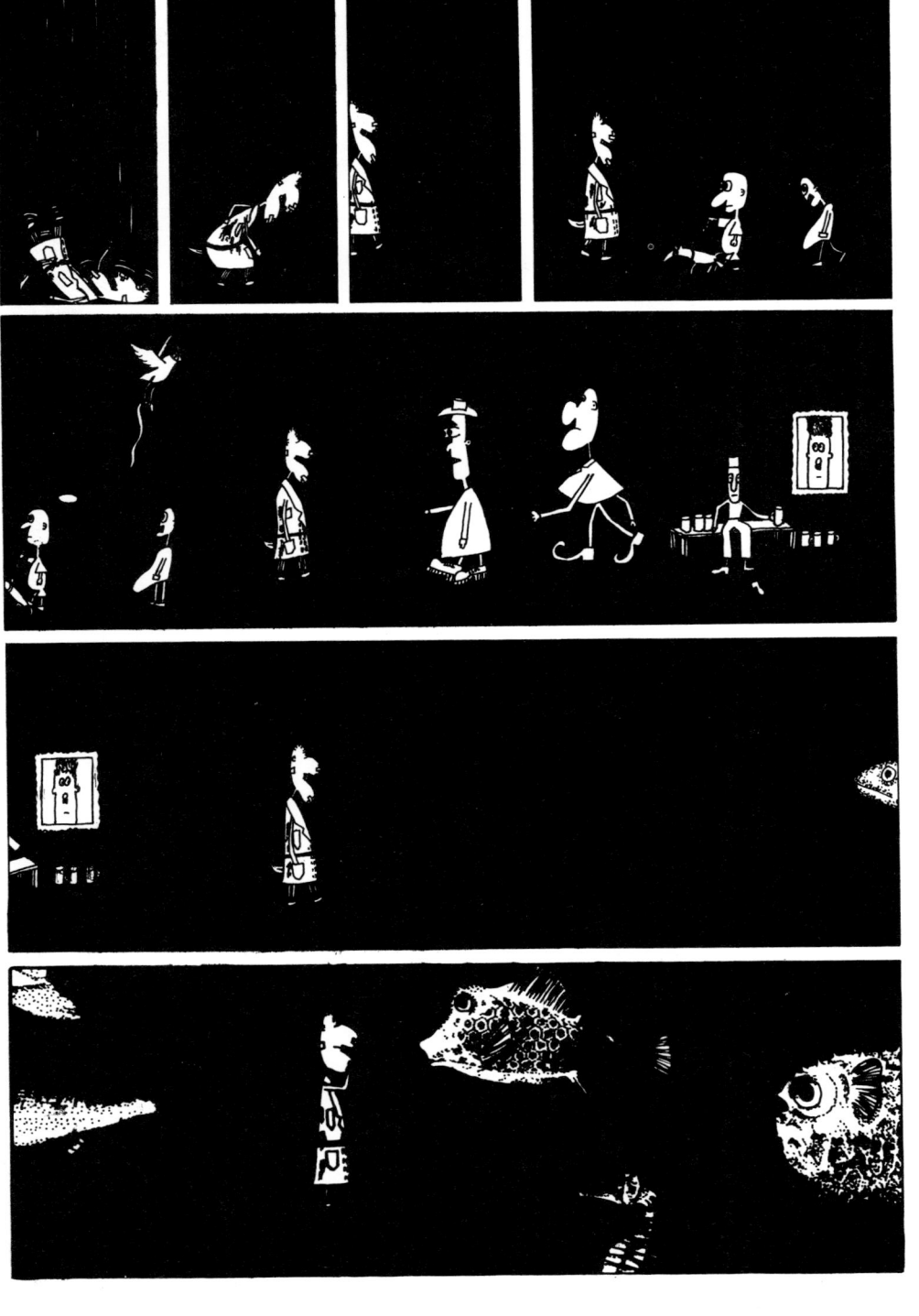

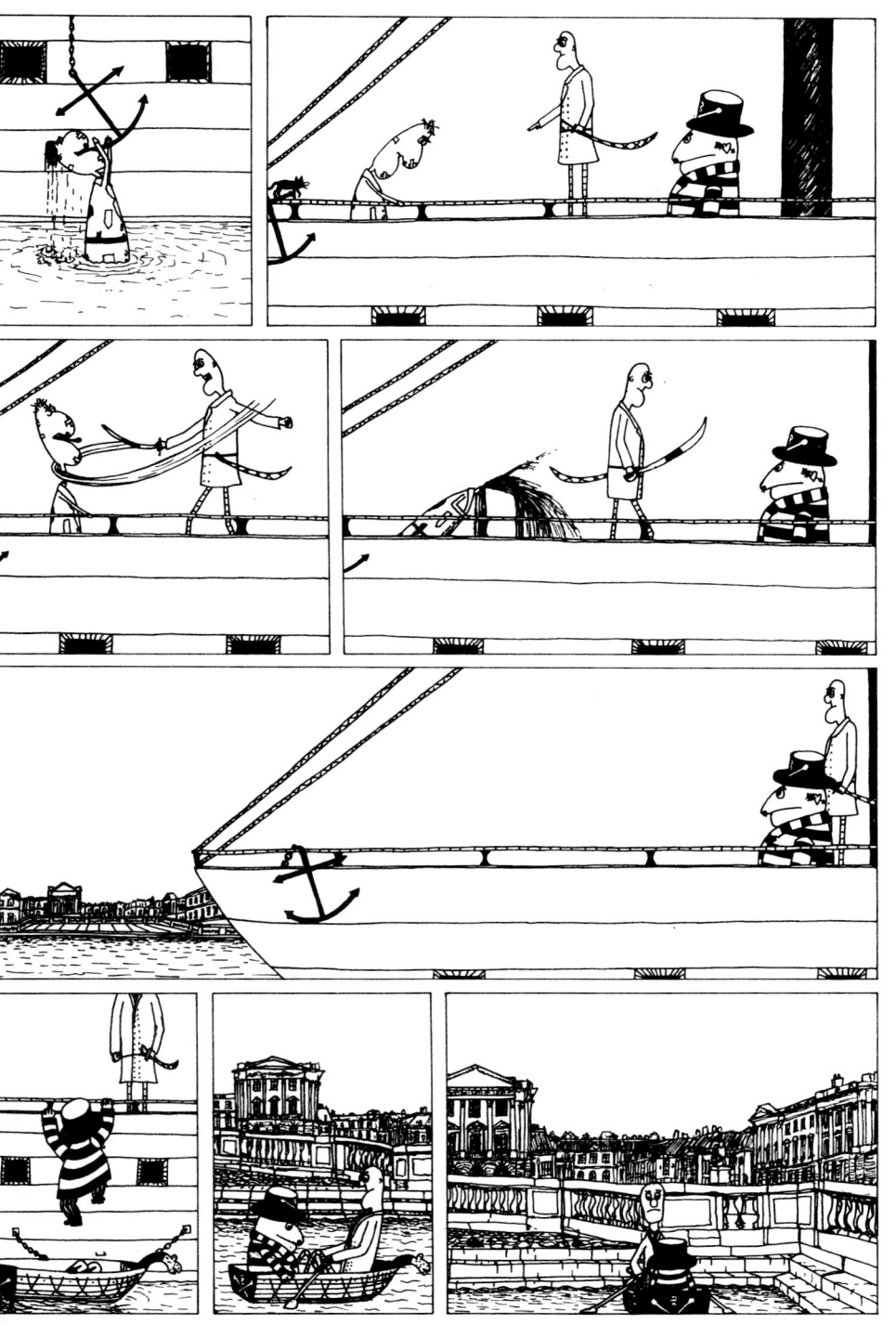

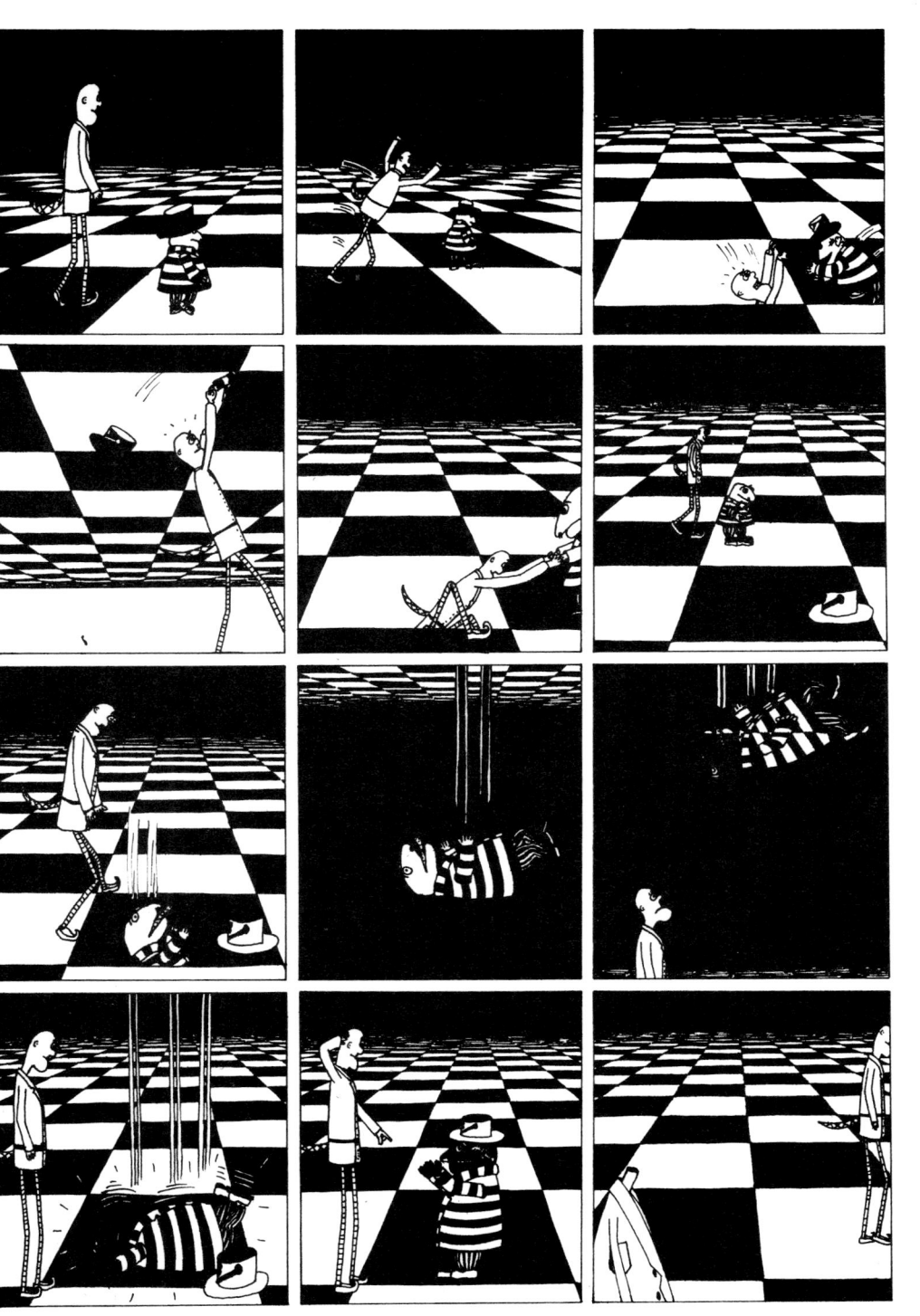

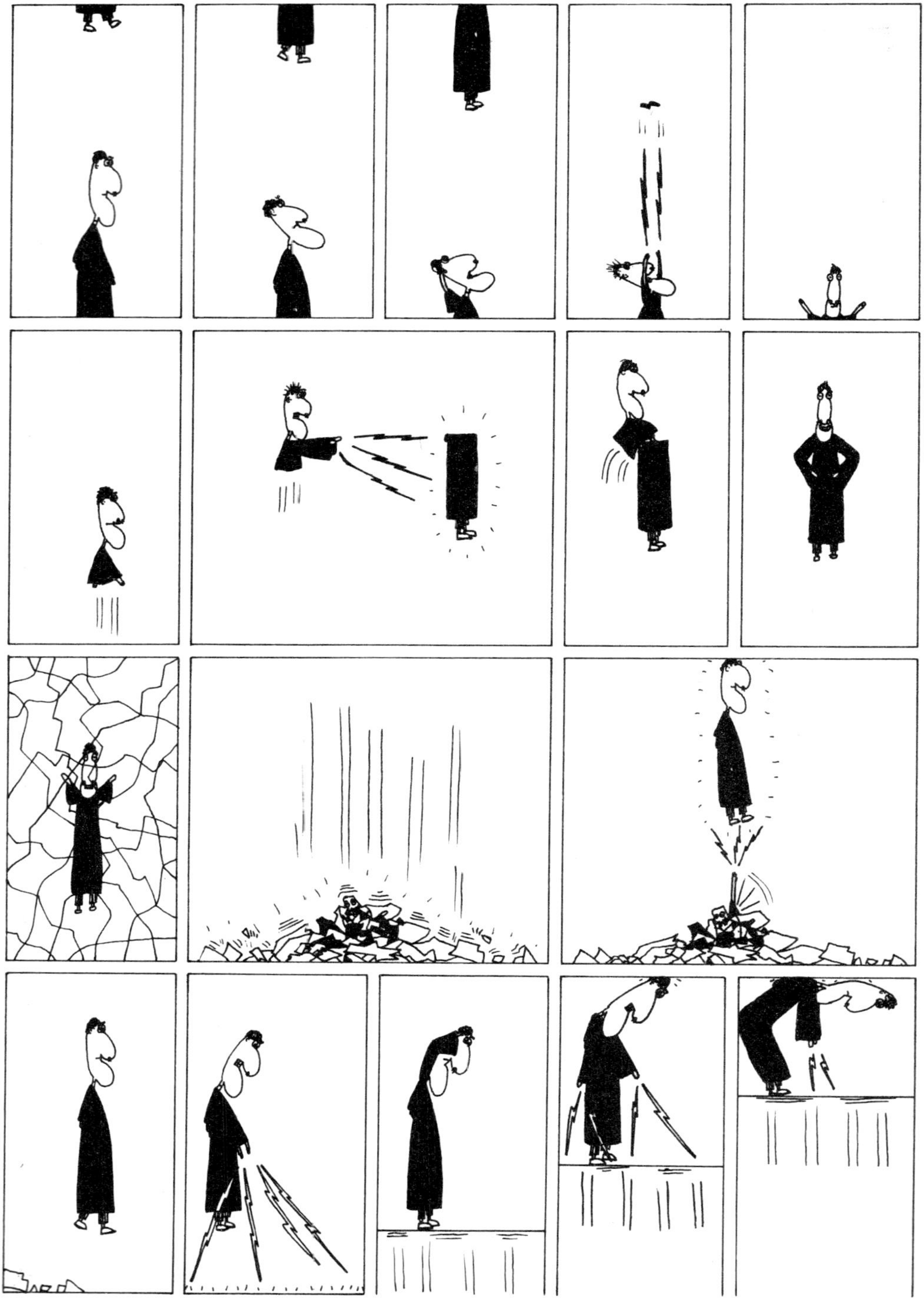

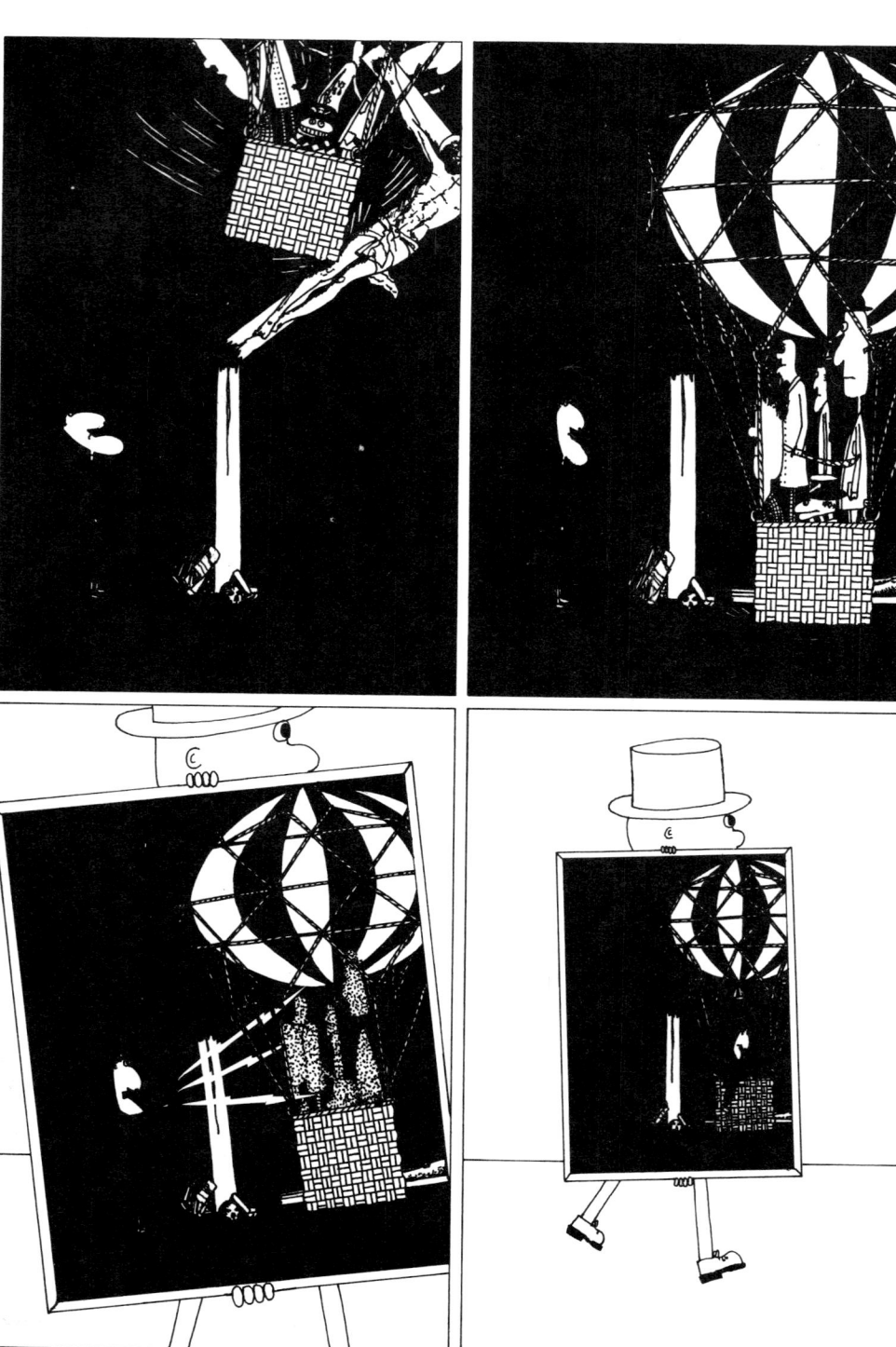

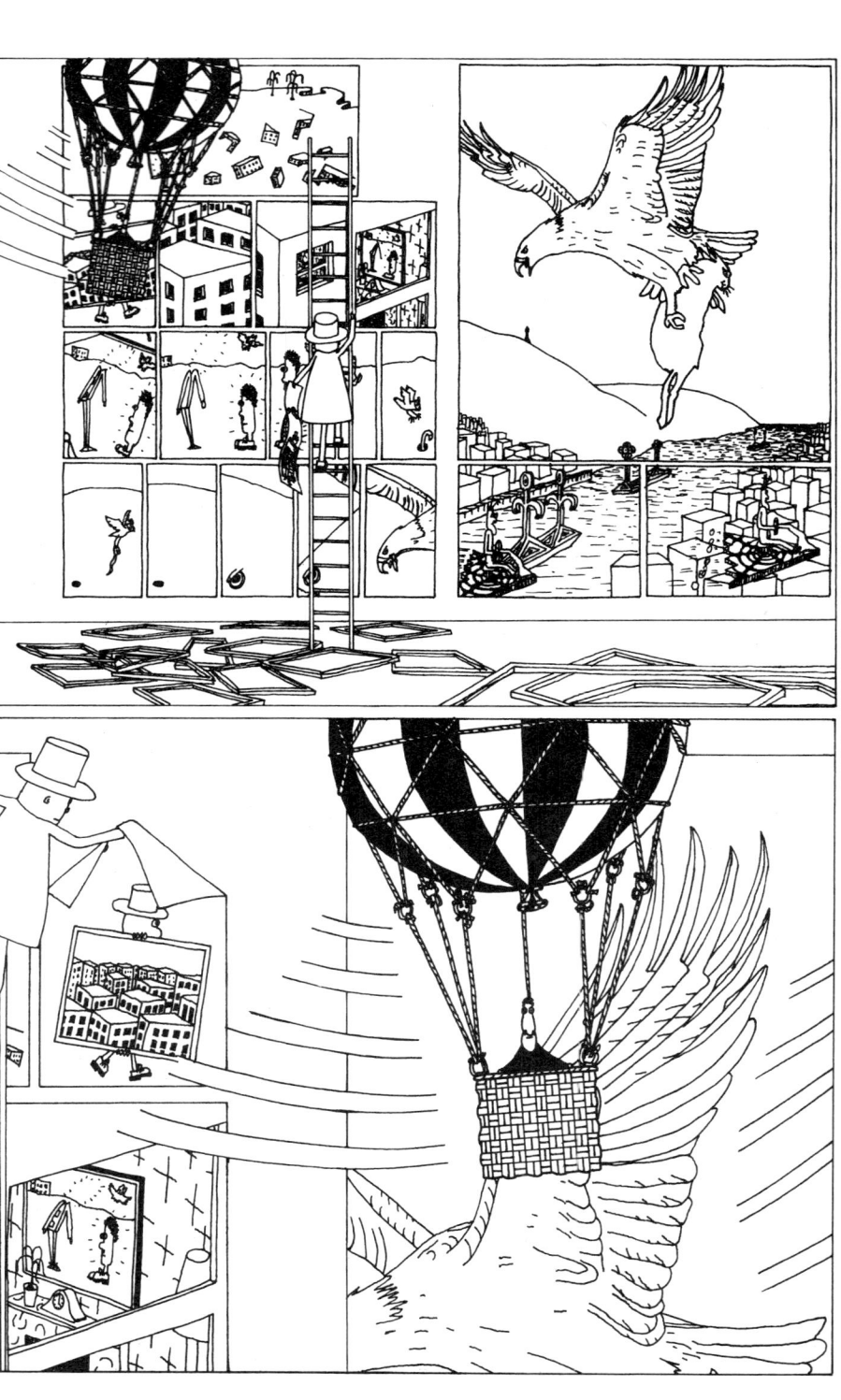